Original title:
The Fruit of Reflection

Copyright © 2025 Creative Arts Management OÜ
All rights reserved.

Author: Elias Marchant
ISBN HARDBACK: 978-1-80586-369-4
ISBN PAPERBACK: 978-1-80586-841-5

Tasting the Essence of Days Past

In the garden where memories play,
I reached for a slice of yesterday.
A peach that whispered, 'Do you recall?
The times we stumbled, how we'd sprawl!'

A banana chuckled, smooth and sly,
'Your past is ripe, oh my, oh my!
Remember that day you danced with glee?
Tripped on your shoelace, oh what a spree!'

An apple grinned with a shiny cheek,
Gave me a wink and began to speak.
'You thought you were cool, wearing stripes,
But a fruit salad's not just for gripes!'

So here I munch on laughter's peel,
Each bite a memory, oh what a deal!
Gone are the sorrows, the frowns misplaced,
In the humor of digestion, joy is embraced!

A Reflection in Each Peel

In the mirror of a citrus,
I see my silly grin,
Peeling back the layers fast,
Finding laughter within.

With each bite, a squeeze of zest,
A pucker and a play,
Life's quirks are all around us,
In a tangy, bright display.

Boughs Heavy with Realizations

The branches bend with wisdom,
Heavy with ripe delight,
Each fruit a goofy secret,
Hanging on with all its might.

Swinging low with heavy thoughts,
They wiggle in the breeze,
I'll gather up the chuckles,
With every giggle, please.

Savoring the Taste of Time

I munch on moments crispy,
Each crunch a tale of fun,
Flavors burst like laughter,
In the warmth of the sun.

Time's a quirky masterpiece,
Painting smiles on each face,
Savoring my goofy thoughts,
At my own snail pace.

The Soft Glow of Knowing

With dimples on an apple,
I find a spark so bright,
Each bite is like a giggle,
Filling up the night.

The glow of silly truths,
In every juicy bite,
Leaves me chuckling softly,
In the dimmest light.

Kiwis of Clarity Under Moonlight

In the garden where shadows play,
Kiwis ponder on what to say.
They giggle and wiggle in the breeze,
Trying to dodge the buzzing bees.

A fruit so fuzzy, yet so wise,
Under moonlight, truth never lies.
They whisper secrets with a peel,
Over ripe thoughts they spin the wheel.

Blooms of Self-Awareness

Daisies dance in a vibrant row,
Each bloom wondering, 'Am I a pro?'
Petals lean in for a gossip spree,
Hoping to solve the great 'who is me?'

Sunflowers nod with silly grins,
While tulips giggle, bursting with sins.
In the garden, clarity grows,
As laughter and absurdity flows.

Orchards of Lost Lullabies

In orchards wide, where dreams collide,
Lost lullabies bounce, and apples hide.
A chorus of fruit sings soft, sweet tunes,
While squirrels dance under silver moons.

Pears ponder where their melody's gone,
While peaches pretend to sing from dawn.
With each bite, a note sweetly resounds,
As giggles ensue in fruity surrounds.

A Mosaic of Colorful Thoughts

Think of bananas with stripes of pink,
In a world where colors dare to wink.
A rainbow of chatter fills the air,
As oranges giggle without a care.

Raspberries blush, feeling quite bold,
While grapefruits gossip stories untold.
A canvas of laughter, each hue a jest,
In this fruit salad, we're all at rest.

Labyrinth of Perspectives

In a twisty maze, I roam and gloat,
Finding wisdom in a floating boat.
A mirror laughs, it shows my face,
I just can't find the right place!

Thoughts like socks, they disappear,
Left behind, oh, what a fear!
In every corner, a giggle hides,
Chasing shadows, my mind abides.

Unspoken Writings of the Heart.

My heart's a book, I dare not read,
A scribbled note, a jumbled seed.
Words tumble out like clumsy cheer,
Oh, could they pen a jest or sneer?

In secret whispers, feelings dwell,
Yet still I trip and cast my spell.
With every laugh, I dodge the truth,
A comical play, my hidden youth.

Whispers in the Orchard

In an orchard where thoughts collide,
Apples giggle with juicy pride.
Lemonade dreams make sour faces,
As laughter rolls in playful races.

Branches sway with silly tunes,
Dancing leaves beneath the moons.
Each whisper tickles ear and mind,
What wisdom's here, I hope to find?

Seeds of Contemplation

Seeds tumble forth, a curious plight,
Some sprout ideas, others just blight.
With cracks and twists they split apart,
Planting giggles in a silly heart.

Each ponder feels like a juggling act,
I wear a crown, but that's a fact!
In every thought, a joke to sow,
Growing laughter, a funny show.

The Essence of Reverie

In the land of fleeting dreams,
Socks and thoughts burst at the seams.
Jumping jacks in a pickle jar,
Chasing giggles, near and far.

Butterflies wear tiny hats,
Whispering secrets to the mats.
Lemonade rivers flow with glee,
Dancing turtles sing to the tree.

Fragments of Truth

Noodles twist like a poet's pen,
Pizza slices fly again.
Globes of cheese bounce on a plate,
Tickling noses, it's just fate.

Chasing shadows of cinnamon,
Fluffy clouds like marshmallow fun.
Silly hats dance on the breeze,
While pickles giggle from the trees.

Blossoms of Solitude

A frog on a log wears a crown,
Cows do somersaults all around.
Invisible friends join the show,
As cupcakes frolic down below.

Jellybeans sing on a swing,
Ants tap dance, what a thing!
While cloud puffs play peek-a-boo,
Giggling softly, "Just us two!"

Tapestry of Inner Landscapes

Beyond the mirror, fish wear ties,
Socks debate over who is wise.
Waffles argue, which is the best,
As pancakes lounge but never rest.

In the woods, where chairs can chat,
Squirrels debate 'bout Mr. Cat.
While candy canes play hide and seek,
And cotton candy whispers, "Peek!"

Meditations in a Cider Jar

Apple cores and laughter spread,
Thoughts that dance, not one in dread.
Bubbles rise like fleeting dreams,
In this jar, nothing seams.

Sticky fingers, a funny chase,
Cider spills all over the place.
Reflections giggle, turning round,
In fruit-filled joy, wisdom found.

Sipping the Essence of Being

Sipping slow, what do I see?
A pear-shaped thought winks back at me.
Lemon zest with a twist of fate,
Life's cocktail, it just feels great!

Cucumber whispers, 'Take a break!'
Mint leaves giggle, 'What's at stake?'
Every sip a little cheer,
Steep my thoughts, it's crystal clear.

Beneath the Canopy of Thought

Hanging branches, ideas ripe,
Coconuts spill, oh what a hype!
Mango smiles under sunny rays,
Shady thoughts, a nutty craze.

Fruits of wisdom drop like rain,
Laughter echoes, never in vain.
Under this leafy, tangled dome,
Find a silly, juicy home.

A Symphony of Mellow Reflections

Bananas play a jazzy tune,
Peaches sway, oh what a boon!
Tomatoes roll across the floor,
In this concert, who needs more?

The apples hum a silly song,
Pineapples dance, they can't go wrong.
Every note, a fruity jest,
In this symphony, we are blessed.

The Bounty of Stillness

In the quiet of the mind, we ponder,
Thoughts as ripe as fruit, we wander.
Ideas bounce like balls in play,
Tickling fancies, in a silly way.

Sitting still, I hear a sneeze,
A thought pops up like leftover cheese.
To reflect is to giggle, oh what fun,
As I chase my shadow under the sun.

The stillness grows, a thoughtful feast,
With every whim, I munch and feast.
Crack open a laugh, a playful quirk,
Finding joy in moments that often lurk.

So here I sit, in my reflective chair,
With snacks of thoughts, both sweet and rare.
Laughter bubbles up like sparkling juice,
In this bounty, I can't help but let loose.

Blossoms of Insight

Oh, the flowers in my head bloom bright,
Tickling thoughts, a silly sight.
Petals of laughter in wacky designs,
Each bloom a giggle, a twist of lines.

Bumbling bees buzz up high,
Chasing thoughts as they fly by.
Stumbling over wisdom's path,
Oh what joy in this silly math.

Each insight bursts like a ripe cherry,
Falling down makes me feel merry.
Swinging from branches of jest and jest,
Is this wisdom? Nah, just my quest.

So I'll dance through the orchard, quite absurd,
In search of the wittiest, silliest word.
With blossoms of insight, I'm feeling spry,
Reflecting and laughing till I fry!

Fragments of Sunlit Memories

In a sunbeam, I reminisce,
Fragments of moments, a comedic bliss.
Each memory's like a tasty treat,
With silly toppings that can't be beat.

Stepping into puddles of yesteryear,
Splashing laughter, nothing to fear.
With every drop, a giggle grows,
Chasing dreams wherever it goes.

The past holds treasures, quirky and fun,
Like unexpected ice cream on the run.
Spilling stories like jam on toast,
I savor the laughter, I laugh the most.

So here's to the sunlit tales we weave,
In the garden of giggles, I truly believe.
Fragments of joy, I gather and stack,
With each chuckle, there's no turning back!

The Orchard of Solitude

In my orchard of thoughts, I twirl,
Alone with giggles, oh what a whirl.
Branches sway with whispers so bright,
As silly shadows dance in delight.

Swinging on swings made of dreams,
With each lofty bound, laughter streams.
Sitting with solitude, I found a mate,
Together we plot mischief, oh, isn't that great?

Nuts and bolts of thoughts parade,
Crafty ideas in sunlight, unmade.
Each chuckle sprouts from a wise little seed,
Oh, reflection is funny, indeed, indeed!

So I frolic through this orchard so fine,
Where solitude mingles with a splash of wine.
With a giggle, a snicker, and a thoughtful cheer,
In my orchard of solitude, it's perfectly clear!

Branches Woven with Wisdom

In the orchard, thoughts do grow,
Like apples hanging, row by row.
Each giggle's a fruit, ripe and round,
Falling softly; wisdom's found.

Grapes of laughter splash the ground,
With each stumble, joy's profound.
A silly dance in grassy lanes,
Harvesting humor through our pains.

Peeling layers with a grin,
Revealing wisdom held within.
Bananas slip, yet never fall,
In laughter's shade, we have it all.

So gather round, let's share a jest,
In this garden, we know best.
A bushel of chuckles waits for you,
Woven dreams, bright and new.

A Tapestry of Ripe Thoughts

In a patch of pondering dreams,
Pineapples poke and peach trees beam.
Ideas bubble like fizzy drinks,
Bathing cheeky minds, in thought springs.

Oranges whisper to the bees,
Sharing secrets with the trees.
Each fruit a thought that dares to roll,
Juicy ideas that fill the soul.

Cherry puns hang by a thread,
Juicy tidbits dance in our heads.
Life's a smoothie, spin it right,
Sipping giggles through the night.

So shake a branch, let laughter rise,
In this patch, the heart flies.
With every bite, our spirits soar,
Tapestries of joy, who could ask for more?

The Garden of Pondering Souls

In the garden where thoughts will sway,
Lettuce giggles in bright array.
Tomatoes blush at silly sights,
Planting jokes in sunny lights.

Cucumbers crunch with witty grace,
Tickle the roots, a merry race.
Every turn, a chuckle waits,
Growing laughter through the gates.

Zucchini dreams float in the breeze,
Spreading cheer with perfect ease.
As we cultivate our funny side,
In this garden, we take pride.

So pull the weeds of worry away,
Let smiles bloom, come what may.
In this patch, souls intertwine,
Harvesting joy, divine.

Juices of Epiphany

Squeeze the day, let laughter flow,
Fruity insights start to grow.
Lemonade dreams tickle the tongue,
As jingles of joy are sweetly sung.

Blend the berries, mix them right,
Sip the silliness, pure delight.
Juicy quirks bubble on top,
Fizzing feelings that never stop.

Peachy wisdom in a cup,
Take a sip, then stand up!
With each gulp, we find our way,
Savoring fun in a zesty play.

So fill your jug with vibrant cheer,
Even ripe figs sway without fear.
In this juice, insights combine,
Finding joy in laughing line.

Twists of the Mind's Vine

In the garden where thoughts abound,
Twisted vines play peek-a-boo,
They giggle and wobble around,
As if they're sharing a joke or two.

Beneath the leaves, a secret lies,
A banana in a berry's suit,
With every glance, a new surprise,
The fruit salad's a funny hoot!

The melons wear their hats askew,
While oranges dance a silly jig,
It's a party of ideas, who knew?
Where laughter is ripe, and minds dig.

So grab a snack, come take a seat,
In this orchard of whimsical cheer,
Where reflections and humor meet,
And the funny fruit always appears!

The Winding Path of Discovery

On paths where thoughts do slowly roam,
Each step reveals a comic clue,
A peanut pretending to be a gnome,
Winks at a squirrel, quite overdo!

A broccoli in shades, oh so bright,
Critiques the wheezy old garden hose,
He bubbles with mirth, what a sight!
As beetroot outsmarts a garden rose!

Outdoor debates of lemon and lime,
Whirling around like a wild dance,
In laughter, they find the best rhyme,
Singing of life and chance in a trance.

So wander down this twisty lane,
With hearty chuckles all around,
Where every silly thought's a gain,
And joy in reflection can be found!

Grapes of Serenity

Tiny grapes, a bunch of cheer,
Whisper secrets only we hear,
They giggle as they dangle low,
Drop some wine, and watch it flow!

In the vineyard of soft delight,
A dappled sun turns day to night,
With every sip, a chuckle grows,
As grapevine humor just overflows.

They jest about the stuffy wine,
And ponder if they could define,
The giggle behind a merry glass,
As laughter ripples through the grass.

So sip and savor, let it spin,
With fruity thoughts, we've got our win,
In the harvest of joy divine,
We pluck the jokes from every vine!

The Candor of Leafy Green

In the shade of leafy trees,
Where spinach tells corny jokes,
The kale rolls on laughing with ease,
While parsley giggles at silly folks.

An avocado sporting shades,
Claims wisdom from the grove above,
While lettuce sings in verdant parades,
Dancing with all the leafy love.

Twirling spinach, bold and bright,
Imparts wisdom in a light cheer,
In this garden, the wit takes flight,
And holds the truth most dear.

So come and join this leafy crew,
Where honesty sprouts with a grin,
When you're silly, the world's askew,
And laughter is where we begin!

Fruits of Quietude

In silence, I try to think,
But my mind is quite the prankster.
Thoughts bounce like rubber balls,
Chasing each other, a wild gang.

I sit still, losing the race,
While squirrels debate my fate.
Maybe they found the secret,
As they chuckle and run away.

A coffee cup in my hand,
The brew is as still as my brain.
Yet the steam rises with such flair,
It pirouettes like it's made for fame.

Amidst songs of chirping birds,
I ponder if they laugh at me.
Do they know the secrets of stillness,
Or fly high, lost in density?

Collecting the Light

I gather sunbeams in a jar,
Hoping they'll brighten my day.
But they tickle and escape,
Laughing at my silly play.

Moonbeams whisper jokes at night,
While stars twinkle with delight.
I shake the jar, that tricky light,
It giggles, oh what a sight!

Candles melt, their waxy tears,
Form stories without a word.
It drips like laughter down the sides,
Sharing secrets absurdly blurred.

But when I open lids too wide,
They scatter like birds on the wing.
What's left in the jar, a glimmer small,
Presents a glow meant for fun things.

Veils of Self-Discovery

Behind the mirror, words collide,
Who is that? Oh, what a ride!
A jester in a crown of thorns,
Making sense of all the yawned.

Each layer pulled, a chuckle heard,
As wisdom wears my favorite shirt.
A wobbling figure, full of glee,
Like a clown hiding in the trees.

Confessions spill like grape soda,
Fizzing up, a bubbly explosion.
Is that honesty buzzing nearby?
Or just my self-doubt in disguise?

I take a bow, applause from me,
As laughter rings more truthfully.
Every veil, a punchline spun,
I find the punch-drunk in the fun!

Pondering Petals

Watching petals fall from grace,
Turning clumsy in their dance.
They tumble like tiny clowns,
Sending giggles with each chance.

The roses sigh in comical tears,
"Why do we bother? Life's a joke!"
Tulips chime with giddy cheer,
"Let's bloom like we're all bespoke!"

Daisies giggle, spinning round,
Whispering fears of roots underground.
"Who cares about the soil's fate?
Let's just bask and celebrate!"

I sit with a grin, watching it bloom,
Each petal a punchline, lifting the gloom.
Life in full color, a floral fête,
Pondering petals, never too late!

Whispers of the Soul

In a garden of thoughts, I trip and tumble,
On my pebbled path, I giggle and grumble.
Chasing shadows of dreams that flutter and fly,
I question the clouds and the laughter up high.

The sun winks at me, oh so sly,
While pondering why the moon's such a spy.
In the pond of my mind, reflections can dance,
With frogs wearing glasses, they take every chance.

I juggle my worries like cats in a hat,
While squirrels play chess with a wise little bat.
Giggles echo loudly, in this whimsical maze,
The whispers of my soul set my heart all ablaze.

Tickles of joy buzz like bees in the breeze,
Sipping on kindness; oh, do what you please.
In this silly adventure, I glow and I glide,
For life's just a laugh when I let go of pride.

Tangled Branches of Memory

In the orchard of yesterdays, ripe fruits dangle,
Each pluck reveals tales that twist and wrangle.
Banana peels laugh as I slip on their plot,
While apples chat loudly, debating a thought.

With pumpkins that ponder and carrots that cheer,
I wrestle with moments, both far and near.
The rhubarb forms teams, in a lively parade,
As tomatoes remind me of the mess I've made.

Thinking back on old follies, they giggle and grin,
In this vineyard of memories, I dance with a spin.
Cabbages clatter in their leafy attire,
As grapes throw a party, fueling my fire.

Through tangled branches, where the sunlight peeks,
I gave my past shenanigans a personality streak.
Every fruit, a reminder, swirling in glee,
In the laughter of life, I find the real me.

Nectar of Introspection

Dripping with sweetness, my thoughts drench the mind,
A honeyed reflection, where giggles unwind.
The bees take a break, sipping wisdom's brew,
While butterflies whisper ridiculous truths.

In this hive of ideas, I bounce and I shuffle,
To the rhythm of laughter, I wiggle and scuffle.
Wasps sipping tea with a curious grin,
Converse about woes from where we've been.

The nectar flows freely; oh what a delight,
A ticklish giggle lasts far into the night.
As I ponder the fuss of all moments I've made,
I find joy in the chaos; the worries all fade.

So here's to the musings that bring out the glee,
Like ants juggling peanuts, so happy and free.
With each little thought, a new chuckle's unwrapped,
In the garden of pondering, I'm quietly trapped.

Boughs of Wisdom

Underneath the trees where the wisdom resides,
I swing from the branches; oh, what a ride!
The squirrels share secrets of the acorn convention,
While the owls roll their eyes at our silly tension.

The leaves dance and flutter, exchanging their news,
While wise-cracking branches offer colorful clues.
"Oh, life's a cacophony of riddle and rhyme!"
They chortle, "But kid, you've got plenty of time!"

A wise old tortoise sets the pace and grins,
While snapping-turtles throw in their quick, funny spins.
With giggles and chuckles, they share all they know,
Writing their stories in the dirt down below.

So join in the laughter that echoes around,
In the boughs of wise trees, let your joy abound.
For wisdom is found in the jester's bright smile,
And often in foolishness, we discover our style!

Pearls of Wisdom in Glistening Dew

In the morning light they gleam,
Thoughts like berries, ripe with dream.
A squirrel stopped, with eyes so wide,
Wondering what wisdom shan't confide.

Jokes in shadows, wisdom clings,
A robin chirps of silly things.
Each droplet holds a secret dance,
A hint of laughter, not just chance.

Pondering life with every sip,
Do fruit-flavored thoughts make one trip?
On branches high, we twist and bend,
Reflecting, and the fun won't end.

Why did the orange blush so bright?
It found its zest in morning light.
Glistening wisdom for all to see,
Share a laugh; come climb with me!

Fruits of Time's Whisper

With whispers soft like evening breeze,
Apples chuckle from the trees.
"Time went where?" they seem to shout,
While giggling leaves dance allabout.

A clock that's tickled, quite absurd,
Makes moments feel like silly birds.
Peaches ponder on yesterday's fun,
While cherries dream of what's to come.

Bananas slip on timeless jokes,
Each laugh a trick by friendly folks.
In the garden, thoughts will sprout,
Time's fruit is sweet, there's never doubt.

So gather round and share a cheer,
For fruits of thought are always near.
In laughter's shade, we find our way,
Whispered fruit brings brighter day!

A Dance of Autumn Leaves

Leaves like laughter, swirling free,
Painting stories on the spree.
In twirls and flips, they show delight,
Season's jests in golden light.

Maples giggle as they sway,
Whispers of summer drift away.
What do you mean—pick me up?
I'm busy dancing, not a pup!

Catch the breeze, join in the jest,
Nature's humor at its best.
With every flurry, every turn,
A leaf proclaims, "Life's full of fun!"

Laughter echoes through the trees,
Antics shared on autumn's breeze.
So grab a leaf and take a spin,
In this merry dance, we all win!

Nectar of the Sage

In ancient groves where wisdom grows,
The sage is known for witty prose.
Sip the nectar, take a chance,
He'll spin a tale that makes you dance.

"Once a grape," he starts to tease,
"Thought it was wise, now look at these!"
With fruity punchlines, quick and sly,
He'll make you laugh till time goes by.

With honey thoughts that tickle your mind,
And tangy truths you'll surely find.
A squeeze of lemon, wise and bright,
Brings giggles in the fading light.

So take a sip and join the swirl,
As laughter blooms and thoughts unfurl.
In every drop, there lies a wink,
Life's sweet nectar makes you think!

Roots of Introspection

In the garden of thoughts, plants grow slow,
Digging deep, where the mind wants to go.
With each silly question, weeds dance in glee,
Finding answers is harder than finding a bee.

Socks on my hands, I ponder the day,
Why do cats always choose to not play?
Moments of wonder, covered in grime,
Like a potato in a tuxedo, just out of time.

Nose in the dirt, I trip on a root,
"Why is the sky different from my boot?"
Twisting thoughts mixed like a well-stirred stew,
I laugh at the mess, it all feels so new.

Yet wisdom grows wild among tickles and laughs,
Like a chicken who thinks it's a horse's past.
Roots twist and turn, in this playful maze,
Finding joy in the funk, in a thousand ways.

Leaves That Speak in Silence

Leaves whisper tales in a gentle breeze,
Tickling the ear, like a child at ease.
Posting secrets from branches up high,
But their punchlines? Oh, they just sigh!

Green wonders wear frowns, so shy and meek,
Like socks on a cat when you play hide and seek.
One leaf hiccups, spilling thoughts on the ground,
And the rest all giggle, "What a silly sound!"

Each leaf holds a chuckle, a quirk, a jest,
Beneath a bright sun, they're all just a mess.
Falling for laughter, they flutter with flair,
Like a dance in a breeze, without a care.

In their rustling banter, stories unfold,
Of a squirrel who thought he was brave and bold.
Leaves chuckle in silence, sharing their tips,
On how to find joy in the quirkiest quips.

Ripe Moments of Clarity

In the orchard of thoughts, fruits ripen slow,
Each one a giggle, just waiting to show.
Bananas in pajamas, oranges with hats,
All waiting for wisdom to rise among chats.

One morning I'm brimming with grape-like delight,
As I ponder if jelly is worth the small bite.
Peaches roll past, with a wink and a grin,
Saying, "Let's dive into chaos and spin!"

A fig in my pocket, a giggly old sage,
Whispers of blunders found on every page.
While lemons just sour on thoughts not quite right,
They squeeze humor into the dazzling light.

When cherries get cheeky and start a small fight,
I laugh till I cry, savoring the bite.
Moments so ripe, bursting forth into play,
Finding joy in the chaos, day after day.

Dappled Light on Wistful Pathways

Dancing shadows fall on the whims of the night,
While twinkling starlight prepares for a flight.
Paths wander off like a cat chasing dreams,
Leading to giggles and outrageous schemes.

A squirrel in a top hat, a raccoon with flair,
Show off their talents, without a care.
Mirth spills like sunlight through trees all around,
Echoing laughter, a whimsical sound.

Wistful reflections on the path that I roam,
Finding laughter in places that feel like home.
With dappled light guiding, I skip and I sway,
Launching into folly, come what may!

So I skip through the darkness, hands held up high,
Embracing the silliness as stars watch the sky.
With every step forward, I chase after glee,
Dappled in laughter, forever so free.

Shadows Beneath the Surface

In puddles deep, the thoughts do dance,
A rubber duck takes its chance.
It quacks a tune, with no one near,
While fish below lend a fin to cheer.

Reflections laugh in shades of green,
A mirror world, oh so serene.
But what's that splat? A bird's delight,
Splashing wisdom left and right.

With every ripple, giggles grow,
As cows on stilts steal the show.
They munch on grass, then slip and slide,
In a muddy dance, with smiles wide.

So come take heed, don't be too shy,
Join the fun beneath the sky.
Where shadows cast their funny tune,
And life's a laugh, like a cartoon.

Garden of Silent Musings

In a patch of dreams, the daisies pout,
While carrots plot with a hidden shout.
Tomatoes roll their eyes with ease,
And lettuce whispers jokes to the breeze.

Among the rows where veggies jive,
A hidden gnome, oh how he thrives!
With funny hats in colors bright,
He juggles pebbles, what a sight!

The sunflowers sway, with silly grins,
As bees buzz in on flowered pins.
"Pollinate me!" they buzz in jest,
While wormy friends claim, "We're the best!"

In this garden, laughter grows,
With every seed that someone sows.
So may your musings dance and twirl,
In this patch, let joy unfurl.

Ripening Insights

An apple fell in a thought parade,
While pears were plotting a grand charade.
"Why did the grape just blush?" they ask,
"Because it saw the juice!" what a task!

Bananas slip, oh what a scene,
With peels bright yellow, shining sheen.
"Maturity's far," they giggle loud,
While oranges roll amidst the crowd.

Melons giggle, while up on high,
With juicy tales that make you sigh.
"Life's a fruit, take a bite!" they yell,
Embrace the juiciness, oh so well!

So ripen up these insights wise,
In fruity laughter, joy will rise.
Life's a harvest, just await,
And share with friends before it's late!

The Orchard of Remembrance

In an orchard sweet, where memories bloom,
Pies float by, giving off room.
With each inhaled, a giggle grows,
As apples tease, "What do you know?"

"Remember when pears wore silly hats?"
"Or danced the tango with the spats?"
Each fruit chuckles, in shades of red,
While nuts with smiles spin tales ahead.

Cherries whisper under leafy hues,
"Let's throw a party, who'll pay the dues?"
The time goes by, but don't you frown,
Each memory's gold, it won't drown.

So join the dance, let echoes swell,
In the orchard where laughter dwells.
Every bite of joy, so fragrant, sweet,
Reminds us how life's truly a treat.

Refined Resilience

A lemon once said with a squeak,
"Life's tough; it can make you weak!"
But when life gives you peels that are sour,
Just toss in some sugar and bloom like a flower.

An apple laughing with a wink,
Said to the pear, "Come, let's think!"
We may roll down a hill, what a sight,
But bruises fade fast, and we're quite light!

Banana in pajamas, dancing away,
Claims it's the best dressed in the fray!
With every slip, it slides with ease,
And giggles along with the rustling trees.

So gather 'round, it's time for jokes,
For even tough times can be bespoke.
With zest and humor, we'll smile and cheer,
In this fruity circus, there's never fear!

The Unearthed Reflection

A carrot once peeked from the ground,
"I've seen things that astound!"
Pigments of earth all mixed with glee,
Reflections on roots, who knew we'd be free?

Potatoes rejoiced with a chuckle so bold,
"Beneath the surface, we're treasures untold!"
With dirt on their faces, they laughed in delight,
Their masks of mud hid their secrets so tight.

Tomatoes turned red at the fickle sun's tease,
"Why blush? It's like wearing a fancy piece!"
In gardens of humor, we'd plant our dreams,
Where life's little lessons burst at the seams.

So let's dig down for the giggles we share,
Laughter is fertile, so let's crop with care.
In this patch of hilarity, sprout we must,
For buried in laughter is the ultimate trust!

Silence Between the Leaves

A whispering breeze nestled in trees,
Said, "Can you hear the fruit's little tease?"
Oranges giggle while hanging about,
In silence, they plan on a zesty shout!

A kiwi converses in soft, muted tones,
"We drape all around, like beautiful drones!"
With ruffled green hats and fuzz on the side,
They giggle at snores of the nearby grape pride.

Oh, how they sway, under moons so bright,
With silent giggles that sparkle at night.
Fruits dance in shadows, a jocular scene,
Where laughter spreads like a soft, comfy green!

So hush now, dear friend, and hear their sweet song,
In the silence, we find where we belong.
Nature's own jesters, so lively and grand,
In the silence of leaves, we'll dance hand in hand!

Journeys into the Heart

A blueberry blushed as it rolled on a trip,
"Adventure awaits, come take a dip!"
The rascal raspberry, quick on its feet,
Said, "Join me, my friend, let's make life a feat!"

They hopped through the orchard, laughing so loud,
Turning heads in the bushes, drawing a crowd.
Mangoes and cherries began to partake,
In a fruity procession, sweet giggles they make.

With paths made of sunshine and laughter so pure,
They journeyed together with hearts that were sure.
In this fruity parade, every moment was gold,
Through bumps and through giggles, their stories unfold.

Let's savor the journey, from start to delight,
Finding joy in the laughter, from day into night.
For in each fruity heart, there's a tale to unfold,
With humor and love, let the adventure be bold!

Harvesting Stillness

In the garden of thought, I tripped on a shoe,
My brain's on a break, but my knees have a view.
The weeds of distraction keep popping their heads,
While I'm trying to figure out what's in my bread.

The sun is too bright, my thoughts start to fry,
A squirrel's bold dance makes me stop and ask why.
I swear he just winked, but maybe I'm wrong,
I'll just join the fun, and sing him a song.

The lettuce is laughing, the tomatoes just roll,
With giggles and chuckles, they're filling my bowl.
A carrot pipes up, "Don't you worry your head,
Just check your reflection in this leafy bed!"

So here I am, plucking thoughts from the vine,
Harvesting humor, where the sun likes to shine.
Who knew introspection could tickle my chin,
In this garden of nonsense, let the fun begin!

Reflections in the Dew

Early morning's gentle, the dew's on parade,
But look! I'm befuddled, my breakfast delayed.
The grass keeps on giggling, it knows that I'm late,
While I'm stuck on a puzzle, I can't even state.

The birds chirp a chorus, they throw in a pun,
"Did you hear about fog? It had quite a run!"
I chuckle and stumble through sparkles of light,
The world's just a jester, all dressed up so bright.

In puddles of laughter, my worries reflect,
The universe winks; it's a mutual respect.
I slip on a dream that's as slippery as dew,
And trip into giggles, oh what a view!

So I gather the glimmers, the quips, and the sighs,
Letting moments of joy tease the clouds in the skies.
With each glinting shimmer, a smile now grew,
In this playful reflection, I'm dancing anew!

Palms of Perception

With palms up to ponder, I swat at a fly,
Who's laughing and buzzing like he's going to cry.
My thoughts like a piñata, swing round and around,
Each poke at my brain brings a sweet, silly sound.

I called out to reason, "Hey, come take a seat!"
But it's stuck in the traffic of its own loud beat.
The jokes and the jests leap from tree to tree,
As I juggle my worries with an air of glee.

In each cranny of laughter, a treasure I find,
Like old-timey cartoons where my thoughts are aligned.
I'm reaching for wisdom, but it's wearing a hat,
With a sign that reads, "Stay light, just imagine that!"

So I shake up my palms and I shout, "Who's in charge?"
As confusion erupts, my perceptions enlarge.
In this circus of whimsy, I'm learning to play,
With palms full of nonsense, I'll brighten my day!

Cultivating Clarity

In the soil of my mind, I plant seeds of jest,
Watered with laughter, they grow with the best.
The weeds try to whisper, "You need to be tense,"
But I tend to my garden with humor that's dense.

In rows of confusion, the carrots now gleam,
While pumpkins are plotting some pie-related scheme.
The radishes wink as they hide under dirt,
"Come join us for snacks; it won't hurt!" they assert.

With a trowel of chuckles, I dig up the quirks,
Exposing the blooms where the giggle-juice lurks.
I toss back my head, and I give them a cheer,
For in this patch of laughter, clarity's near.

When harvest time comes, I'll feast on delight,
With veggies so funny, they bring such insight.
I'll take a big bite of my own silly fruit,
And dance in the garden, where joy takes root!

The Core of Gentle Wisdom

In the garden of thought, where ideas grow,
Seeds of silliness begin to sow.
A pear with a joke, ripe and round,
Giggles and laughter are easily found.

Underneath the shade of an apple tree,
A worm tells a tale, oh so free!
He wiggles and wriggles, with a wink and a grin,
Sharing his secrets, let the fun begin!

Cherries chuckle as they swing on their stems,
Witty little orbs, crafting whims and gems.
Jokes fly about like butterflies bright,
Making good sense of the silliest plight.

With every bite of wisdom so sweet,
The laughter lingers like a tasty treat.
So pluck a thought and share it today,
For joy in reflection is the best kind of play!

Blossoms Dancing on a Breeze

Petals take flight, with a giggle or two,
Dancing through daylight, wearing bright dew.
They twirl and they twist, on a gentle spree,
A ballet of colors, wild and free.

Tulips gossip, sharing tales on the wind,
Whispering secrets, where laughter's been pinned.
A daisy trips over its own cheery face,
Spreading joy as it tumbles, a clumsy grace.

Snapping at clouds, the lilacs all cheer,
Their sweetness a song that all want to hear.
Each blossom a comedian, brightening days,
In a world of reflection, where humor plays.

As the breeze tickles petals, chuckles abound,
With bursts of delight in the dance all around.
So waltz with some blossoms, let your heart sway,
In the laughter of life, find joy in the play!

Lavender Thoughts in a Honey Jar

Sipping on sweetness from a jar full of dreams,
Where lavender whispers and silliness beams.
A bee cracks a joke about flowers and rain,
Buzzing with laughter, it's all in the brain.

Honey drips down, sticky and warm,
Sticky thoughts linger, a delightful swarm.
With each spoonful, a chuckle is shared,
Seriousness sneaks out, feeling quite dared.

A butterfly chuckles, painting the sky,
Tickling the lilies, making them sigh.
Gardens are giggling, all ages and hues,
For laughter's the nectar that everyone proves.

So dip in the honey, taste every cheer,
With lavender hugs to disperse every fear.
In jars of reflection, let humor roam free,
For joy is the essence of life's honeybee!

Petal-Pushing Through Mindscapes

Mindscapes bloom where thoughts take their flight,
Petals push forth, igniting delight.
A sunflower grins, tight-lipped and bold,
Teaching the lesson that laughter can't be sold.

In the maze of ideas, twisty and fun,
Petals navigate paths, dancing in the sun.
A rose tells a pun, with a thorn in its side,
While lilies laugh softly, they simply can't hide.

Carnations conspire, planning their spree,
A comedy sketch near the old oak tree.
With each silly wink and a clever reprise,
They sprinkle the air with giggles and sighs.

So petal-push onward, through highs and through lows,
In the garden of genius where humor just grows.
Reflect on the jokes that the blossoms bestow,
For life blooms in laughter, as we learn and we grow!

Harvest of Thoughts

When pondering deep, I trip on my shoes,
My thoughts run wild, yet I still snooze.
Bananas of wisdom hang from the tree,
While oranges joke, 'Just peel and see!'

Grapes of ideas all squished in a bowl,
One steals the show and begins to roll.
Strawberries laugh at their own red hue,
They stick together, like me and my stew!

A melon chimes in, what's ripe in your mind?
Kiwis just giggle, they're always so kind.
With each juicy laugh, new thoughts take flight,
Harvesting humor, it feels just right!

So here's to the journey, the quirky spree,
When pondering life, just slip on some glee.
I'll gather my thoughts, a buffet for all,
In this zany garden, I'll stand tall!

Echoes from Within

In the chamber of my crowded head,
Echoes bounce like they're dancing instead.
A pea in a pod sings a silly song,
While carrots debate if they're right or wrong.

A voice whispers softly, "Let's make a stew!"
But the cherries just giggle, and argue for blue.
Each echo a laugh trapped under my hat,
While lemons just pucker, "We're zestier, stat!"

Reflections abound in this playful maze,
Tomatoes are blushing, caught in a gaze.
"Who's there?" asks an apple, "Is it just me?"
"Let's toast to our wisdom, just wait and see!"

The echoes keep bouncing, all jumbled and bright,
It's a fruit salad party, and oh what a sight!
In this weird little space, I find my delight,
With laughter and banter, I dance through the night!

Seeds of Contemplation

Planting some thoughts in a patch of my mind,
Wandering seeds sprout, both silly and kind.
A pumpkin once told me to lighten my load,
While pickles all joked, "Let's spice up the road!"

Tomatoes are pondering, "What comes next, then?"
"Let's ketchup to fun!" shouts a radish, and then.
All sprouts start to giggle, the corn starts to sway,
With jokes and jests keeping the weeds at bay.

Grapefruit pops up, "What's sour makes sweet,"
As it cracks up at all of our clumsy feet.
In this garden of giggles, I'm planting with care,
Watering laughter, let the sunshine flare!

So, sowing some seeds of thought in the ground,
We harvest connection, that's truly profound.
Together we grow, sharing sunlight and cheer,
In this patch of reflections, I hold you dear!

Mirror of the Mind

Peering into the glass, what do I see?
A reflection of antics, just wild as can be.
Funny faces staring, each winks with a grin,
As they jostle and giggle, their dance can begin.

A cantaloupe smirks, "You're looking quite ripe!"
While a mischievous berry declares, "You're hype!"
Mirroring moments, they twist and curl,
Each ponder brings laughter, a whimsical whirl.

"Who let the oranges out?" the bananas shout loud,
While broccoli struts, feeling all kinds of proud.
Reflecting on laughter, it echoes like sound,
In this vibrant realm, joy knows no bound.

So here in this mirror, I find a sweet truth,
Joy dances and sparkles, a fountain of youth.
Amidst all the fun, let's raise our minds high,
For laughter's the treasure, it's never a lie!

The Path of Mindful Harvesting

In a garden of thoughts so bright,
I tripped on a weed, what a sight!
Plucking laughter from vines so green,
Sowed seeds of joy in the unseen.

With each step, I danced like a fool,
Waving at shadows, breaking the rule.
Picking thoughts that were ripe with glee,
Harvesting smiles from the old oak tree.

Bananas wearing hats, oh so quaint,
Apples in sunglasses, looking like paint.
Every moment a giggle, a jest,
On this path, absurdity's best.

So I gather these whims, in a basket so wide,
Happiness bouncing like a carnival ride.
Mindful of nonsense, I walk on air,
Laughing at life, without a care.

Conversations with Stillness

Whispers of silence, a chat with a breeze,
Talking to daisies, they do as they please.
A dialogue deep with a rock and a snail,
Both sharing secrets of their slow trail.

I asked the clouds what they think of the sun,
They giggled and floated, then said, "We're just fun!"
Leaves chimed in with a rustling cheer,
"Just hang with us, nothing to fear!"

With stillness around, I chuckled so loud,
As an ant took a stroll, feeling quite proud.
Conversations abound in this quiet retreat,
Even the mushrooms are tapping their feet.

So join the discourse with a grin on your face,
Nature's comedians, we're all in the chase.
Hilarity reigns in each sound and each sight,
Laughing with stillness from morning to night.

Sweetness Found in Quiet Lands

Wandering through meadows, a curious quest,
Found a chocolate fountain, sweetened my rest.
Butterflies joined in a sprinkle parade,
Mixing slide and giggles, a joyful charade.

Lollipops growing from trees in a line,
Sticky fingers pointing, "Look! What a sign!"
Every step taken, a sugary crunch,
Sipping on nectar, oh what a brunch!

The sun chimed in with a jelly bean glow,
While flowers debated which flavor to show.
Sweetness abounds in this land of delight,
Where even the humor has taken a bite.

So let's play tag with the breeze that we find,
In quiet realms where laughter, unbinds.
Savoring sweetness from morning till dusk,
Life is a candy, a sugary musk.

The Harvest of Forgotten Dreams

In a field overgrown with wishes gone pale,
I stumbled on visions, each one a tale.
Chasing a shadow that danced on my sleeve,
Harvesting giggles from thoughts that believe.

Forgotten dreams hid under the hay,
I teased out their laughter, made my own play.
Each whim a surprise, a puzzle to crack,
Turned sighs into snickers, no looking back!

A smile from a sunflower, oh what a prank,
Twirling in circles with a mischievous flank.
All around, the echo of chuckles resound,
In the harvest of dreams, pure joy can be found.

So gather these giggles, let them take flight,
In the sunshine of mirth, every moment feels right.
From dreams of the past, new laughter will spring,
The harvest of folly is the best kind of bling.

Sunshine Woven into Memory

Sunshine sparkles on my nose,
As I ponder yesterday's woes.
A laugh escapes, a chuckle so bright,
Did I really wear socks with sandals in sight?

Chasing shadows, I trip on a shoe,
Thinking of all the silly things I knew.
How did my dance moves ever get so wild?
Turns out they were made for a circus child!

A banana peel lies on the floor,
Reminding me of days I can't ignore.
Was it me who slipped, or fate's cruel jest?
Sugar on top? Oh, I'll take the rest!

So here's to laughter, a joyful twirl,
In a garden of memories, let joy unfurl.
With each grin shining like dew on grass,
I'll weave my sunbeam, hoping this won't pass!

The Pomegranate of Past Lives

Oh, pomegranates and their juicy delight,
Each seed a giggle, memories in flight.
Did I really wear that neon pink coat?
Or was it a target for bees on a boat?

Slipping past lives like a cloak that sways,
I see myself in imaginative ways.
Was I a pirate, a cat in disguise?
Or a cactus with arms waving 'hi' to the skies?

Counting seeds, oh, what a chore,
Why did I think I could stuff in one more?
Coughs and splutters mark my playful snack,
With each juicy laugh, there's no turning back!

In this garden of dreams, I swing with glee,
Pondering past lives, so wild and free.
As I munch on my bounty, I toss out a grin,
What if the next life's a jolly old spin?

Threads of Gold in Evening Light

As the sun dips low, I find my thread,
Stitching tales of laughter, where giggles spread.
Did I really think I could dance on the sun?
With a wink and a belly flop, I consider it fun!

Woven golden rays like spaghetti twist,
Remind me of moments I used to insist.
That my cat could sing opera, oh what a voice,
But all it meowed was its own tough choice!

The fabric of dusk whispers secrets so sly,
Twinkling like stars making mischief in the sky.
Did I just wear polka dots at the gala?
Oh dear, my fashion's a comical story, not a saga!

So gather your threads, let's quilt this delight,
Each stitch a memory, sparkling and bright.
With laughter sewn tightly through each funny seam,
We weave our tales in the golden beam!

The Lullaby of Garden Shadows

In the garden where shadows play,
Laughter dances the night away.
Did I really scold the gnomes with a broom?
They simply shrugged, saying, 'We live in your room!'

Frogs croak lullabies under the moon,
While crickets join in, a silly tune.
Was that a squirrel attempting a hop?
Or just my neighbor, giving it a flop?

With each rustling leaf, giggles arise,
Echoing softly, revealing the skies.
Late-night reflections, quite absurd at best,
Who thought a cabbage could wear a crown and jest?

So here in the shadows, we sway without care,
In a world of antics, so wondrous and rare.
Join this funny symphony, let laughter abide,
As the echoes of twilight our joy cannot hide!

Ripened Thoughts Under the Stars

Under the cosmos, thoughts collide,
Like fireflies dancing, with nowhere to hide.
Laughter spills out, a sweet, silly game,
As goofy ideas take on new names.

The moon chuckles softly, a wink in the night,
While dreams on a comet shoot up with delight.
Stars sip their tea, in a pearly mug,
As we ponder the absurd, and give it a hug.

Egos get tangled, like spaghetti on plates,
While wisdom does cartwheels and evokes funny fates.
With every giggle, a thought takes a spin,
Ripe laughter awakens the joy deep within.

So dance with your musings, let mischief ignite,
In this garden of laughter, the world feels so bright.
Under the stars, let's not take a stand,
For thoughts that are ripe, can slip through your hand.

Cherries of Understanding

Plump cherries dangle on wisdom's tall tree,
With giggles and snorts, they invite you and me.
Each bite brings a chuckle, a juicy delight,
As truths become jokes—oh what a sight!

Stacking these berries, we find room for more,
Unruly ideas spill out on the floor.
They roll like marbles, all shiny and red,
Leaving us chuckling over what's said.

In this orchard of folly, we pluck what we need,
Sipping the nectar that laughter can breed.
Juicy revelations pop like confetti,
Who knew that reflection could come out so witty?

So let's munch on these cherries, in playful retreat,
As wisdom and humor go hand in hand sweet.
Each quirky insight, we'll cherish and keep,
In the garden of giggles, our minds take a leap.

Gentle Rains on Reflective Days

Drizzles of pondering, soft as a sigh,
With each drop, a chuckle floats into the sky.
Umbrellas of laughter bloom all around,
In puddles of wisdom, joy is unbound.

Each raindrop a riddle, each splash a surprise,
While thoughts drown in giggles, from our silly ties.
We jump in the puddles, our worries all float,
As reflection taps lightly, like rain on a boat.

The clouds overhead giggle, a ticklish breeze,
Encouraging silliness, putting minds at ease.
So let's splash through the water, come dance in the wet,
On reflective days, who could ever forget?

With puddles of laughter, we'll sail on this stream,
Riding the waves of our whimsical dream.
As raindrops keep falling, they spark our delight,
In a gentle downpour, everything feels right.

Almond Blossoms in the Heart

Almond blossoms flutter, so sweet and so light,
Twirling to giggles that take off in flight.
They whisper to us secrets in breezy prance,
As we ponder the art of a spontaneous dance.

In every pink petal, a chuckle might bloom,
Sending joy just like nutty perfume.
Reflective and silly, our laughter takes root,
With each hearty giggle, we shake off the soot.

Blossoms of thinking, like candy for thought,
Rolling around in the jests they have taught.
In this orchard of madness, let's twirl and spin,
With almonds of wisdom, let the fun begin!

So gather the laughter, let's enjoy this show,
Where blossoms of humor in our hearts overflow.
As blooms fill the air with a joyful embrace,
In this garden of love, we'll find our own place.

Shadows Beneath the Apple Tree

Underneath the apple tree,
I found a thought just chilling.
It wore a hat and shades you see,
And kept on laughing, silly.

It told me jokes about the pears,
And danced around with zeal.
I wondered if it knew my fears,
But all it did was squeal.

The worms were joining in the fun,
Their wiggles made me giggle.
A picnic party just begun,
With apples for a wiggle.

So here beneath this leafy shade,
Life's weight felt lightly crushed.
With jokes and laughter all displayed,
To joy, I happily rushed.

Echoes of Silent Thoughts

In the quiet of my head,
Thoughts take turns and play a game.
One's a dancer, one's a shred,
And both can't seem to tame.

They bounce around like rubber balls,
Creating echoes, loud and clear.
I trip, I fall, I laugh, it sprawls,
Is anyone else near?

The clock ticks slow but thoughts run wild,
Making faces at my brain.
I'm just a curious, silly child,
With musings gone insane.

So here I sit, all in a spin,
With echoes strong and bright.
In this chaotic whirl, I grin,
Embracing sheer delight.

Harvest of Inner Dreams

In fields where funny visions sprout,
My dreams are ripe and ready.
I pick them like a silly scout,
While holding on to steady.

A dream of flying with a cat,
Then skiing down a hill,
Another one with a hat,
That cooks with perfect skill.

I gather all my wacky schemes,
And stack them like a tower.
I smile at all these whims and dreams,
In this bizarre flower.

So munching on my dream-filled pie,
I laugh at life's sweet joke.
With every wild thought on the fly,
I'm grateful—what a poke!

Nectar of the Mind's Eye

In my mind's eye, bubbles float,
Filled with nectar, oh so sweet.
I poke and pop, oh what a joke,
   Each splash is quite a treat.

One bubble holds a dancing bee,
   The other a funny clown.
With giggles shared by you and me,
   We wear our laughter crown.

The nectar spills, it drips and flows,
   Creating puddles of delight.
We splash around as laughter grows,
   In this whimsical flight.

So come and taste this silly brew,
   Each sip brings more of me.
In bubbles bright and laughter true,
   Life's fun, can't you see?

Sweets of Late-Night Reverie

In the fridge, there hides a pie,
A midnight feast that I can't deny.
With whip-cream clouds and chocolate flares,
I tiptoe slowly, hoping no one stares.

I freshen my breath with minty gum,
As I lift the slice, feeling quite numb.
'It's fruit,' I whisper, 'healthy and neat,'
While stuffing my face, oh what a treat!

The clock strikes two, my binge is done,
My belly now feels like a giant stun.
I smile with crumbs stuck in my cheek,
In this fairy tale, I'm the laughing freak.

So here's to snacks that light the night,
In shadows, we munch till morning light.
We laugh and feast with glee in our eyes,
In late-night silliness, our spirits rise.

Illumination Amongst the Boughs

Underneath the apple tree, I sit,
A squirrel leers, giving me a jittery fit.
He chats with branches, quite the loud whiz,
While I ponder if fruit snacks count as a quiz.

The pears dangle low, a tempting sight,
A game of dodge as I run in fright.
With every step, they swing and sway,
As I laugh at how they dance away.

A banana peels back, as if to tease,
"Come on, friend, join us, have some cheese!"
But I just giggle, give my head a shake,
No cheese for me, just pie and a cake!

So tangled we get in silly delight,
The fruits all giggle, oh what a sight!
With every chuckle and every fall,
I roam the orchard, embracing it all.

Paths of Twisted Grapevines

Tangled in vines, I trip and spin,
A grape's hidden laugh, oh where to begin?
With a slip and a slide on slippery ground,
Nature's bold prank, I tumble around.

The grapes have conspired, oh what a team,
Hiding their fruit like a devious scheme.
"Catch us if you can!" they bubble and tease,
As I chase them down, falling to my knees.

My friends all laugh, it's a slapstick show,
While I grapple with harvests, row by row.
With each juicy pop, I'm met with a cheer,
As I taste the mischief, I grin ear to ear!

So here's to the vines that twist and shout,
Creating sweet chaos, there's no doubt.
With echoes of laughter in summer's heat,
We dance through the patches, this life is sweet.

The Still Water of the Orchard

By the pond, I spy a splash,
With lily pads floating, making a dash.
Reflections of fruit in a wobbly dance,
While frogs croak rhythms, lost in a trance.

An orange whispers, "Hey, look at me!"
With a wink and a nudge, as bold as can be.
A peach pipes up, quite proud of its fluff,
While I chuckle, thinking, "This is enough!"

The mischief unfolds, a fruit masquerade,
With plums in tuxedos, all finely displayed.
They twirl on the water, dressed to impress,
As I giggle loudly, elated by mess.

In stillness, we find moments so bright,
Where echoes of laughter mingle with light.
So here's to the scenes where we play and jest,
In the pond's silent wisdom, we're truly blessed.

Juicy Insights from Life's Tree

Life hangs low, like fruits on a vine,
Sometimes I pick the ones that don't shine.
Biting into wisdom, a funny surprise,
Tasting the truth, while wearing a guise.

Peeling back layers, I find what I crave,
A laugh with each slip, oh how I wave!
Sweetness and tang blend in my grin,
Each lesson a chuckle, where do I begin?

Fruits of my folly drop all around,
Some turn to jelly, and others unbound.
I savor each bite, though some make me cringe,
A comedic twist on life's silly hinge.

In this orchard of thought, I swing and I sway,
Finding joy in the slips, come what may.
So here's to the laughter, the joys and the pain,
For each fruit of insight brings wisdom again.

Petals of Personal Truth

Petals flutter down from branches of jest,
Each fold a secret, a humorous quest.
I gather them lightly, as if they were snacks,
Tasting their flavors, with giggles and hacks.

In gardens of laughter, I plant my own seed,
Twirling around with no worry or greed.
The blooms all around me, a riotous sight,
Personal truths bursting, what a delight!

With colors that pop, so vibrant and fun,
Each petal a story, when shared, they just stun.
A bouquet of blunders, arranged with great flair,
Sprinkled with laughter, it fills up the air.

So next time you ponder the petals you find,
Remember the giggles, be light-hearted and kind.
For wisdom can blossom in ways we don't see,
And laughter, my friend, is the key to be free.

The Aroma of Silent Revelations

In the still of the night, scents drift through the air,
Whispers of wisdom, like jokes without care.
I sniff at the sweetness, the flavors that tease,
Each breath a chuckle, a moment of ease.

The aroma of laughter hangs thick in the room,
As I stumble through thoughts like a cartoonish bloom.
Silent revelations, they pop up, oh dear!
With each roguish whiff, I dissolve into cheer.

Essences linger of lessons well learned,
Spritzed with humor, my mind gently turned.
So many funny facts tucked under the skin,
Like spices of life, let the fun begin!

In this fragrant dance, I sway side to side,
Each revelation a tickle, a joyous ride.
Collecting these scents, my heart feels so light,
For laughter's the recipe that makes life just right.

Seeds Bursting with Possibility

Tucked in the soil, the seeds start to grin,
With possibilities sprouting, let the fun begin!
Bursts of surprise, they sprout through the earth,
Each laugh is a seed, giving life a new birth.

I toss in my whims, with a flick and a spin,
Creating a garden where humor can win.
The sprouts all around me, a colorful crew,
Each one a reminder of what joy can do.

Some grow into trees, while others are shy,
Yet all share the gift of a giggle nearby.
In fields of uncertainty, I skip and I dance,
Each seed, a new chance, a whimsical chance.

So plant your own dreams in this life of surprise,
And laugh with the seeds that burst into skies.
With every new sprout, let your laughter unfurl,
For life's a grand harvest, a comedic whirl.

www.ingramcontent.com/pod-product-compliance
Lightning Source LLC
Chambersburg PA
CBHW070007300426
43661CB00141B/292